Let's Read the Noah's Ark Story

For Jay and Danny   A.A.

Text by Lois Rock
Illustrations copyright © 2001 Alex Ayliffe
This edition copyright © 2004 Lion Hudson

The moral rights of the author and illustrator
have been asserted

A Lion Children's Book
an imprint of
Lion Hudson plc
Mayfield House, 256 Banbury Road,
Oxford OX2 7DH, England
www.lionhudson.com
ISBN 0 7459 4905 3

First edition 2004
1 3 5 7 9 10 8 6 4 2 0

A catalogue record for this book is available
from the British Library

Typeset in 32/46 Kidprint MT Bold
Printed and bound in Singapore

**This Bible tale is adapted from the story of Noah,
which can be found in Genesis, chapters 6–9**

let's read the
Noah's Ark Story

Retold by Lois Rock ✷ Illustrated by Alex Ayliffe

LION
CHILDREN'S

Old Man Noah listens,
he hears the voice of God . . .

'My world has all gone bad;
I'm going to wash it in a flood.

'So build an ark, long, wide and high, your family and you...

'And on it take the animals,
by two, by two, by two.

'Fetch all the creatures of
the wild – the rabbit,
deer and shrew...

'The tiger and the elephant,
the snake and Kangaroo.

'Then every kind of bird must come, to fill the ark with song.'

When Noah has them safe
on board, it rains both
hard and long.

For days the big ark floats
away, then BUMP –
it hits a peak.

A dove flies out, and then
comes back, a green leaf
in its beak.

The waters trickle to the sea;
at last the land is dry.

God says, 'The flood is over.
See – my rainbow in the sky.'

Other titles in this series from
Lion Children's Books

0 7459 4904 5

0 7459 4932 0